The Rome I Love

THE ROME I love...

Photography by PATRICE MOLINARD

Introduction by JEAN GIONO

Titles by FÉLICIEN MARCEAU

Text by GEORGES PILLEMENT

Translated by RUTH WHIPPLE FERMAUD

TUDOR PUBLISHING COMPANY
New York

Jean GIONO

MY FIRST TRIP to Rome was with Antoine, a friend who is just as unpredictable as I am. From Civita-Vecchia on we expected to see Rome. We felt that a city worthy of that name was obliged, for its own sake and ours, to occupy the horizon like a shimmering beacon. All we saw was a desert the color of a straw doormat.

Antoine finally decided that we had made a mistake. Since I was supposedly the navigator, I pointed out that we had come to no crossroads except the Magliana road which very obviously did not lead to the capital of the world and that, besides, the milestones said: ROMA, 18 kilometers. "Well," he said, "what do you think of that?" — "I don't." During this time we were shooting the chutes in the middle of a waste of sand dunes; we went down into suffocating depths where a few dusty elms were hiding; we climbed up bare hummocks from which we still saw nothing but the desert.

Roma, 4 kilometers. This time the joke had gone on long enough. We stopped and asked ourselves, "Who do they think they're kidding? And what's so clever about that?" On second thought, maybe it *was* kind of clever: look at the state we were in. A hundred Babylonians huddled at our feet couldn't have perplexed us more.

We set off again nice and easy, our eyes peeled, saying to ourselves: "Old girl, you can't fool us. Four kilometers isn't the end of the earth, you've got to be somewhere."

Suddenly we landed between a formidable wall and a row of houses, gasping as at the end of a rollercoaster ride (and yet it wasn't a steep hill) and we found ourselves down below in a mass of cars, horsedrawn carriages and motor-scooters circling around a policeman clad from head to toe in a uniform as white as a sheet. We were so confused that we continued to drive around him for at least ten minutes until, irritated by our stubbornness and our bewilderment, he shooed us on with a wave of his hand (a Roman wave, at that) and Antoine obeyed at once. We parked the car in front of a terrace café.

We had promised ourselves all sorts of off-beat drinks: we ordered two beers. My friend said; "Ha! Well now, this is Nîmes." — "What is Nîmes?"— "Your Rome." — "So now this city is mine?" — "Yes, plane trees, cafés and absolutely nothing at all. It's Nîmes." He drank his beer.

It's true that the place had nothing extraordinary about it. A mid-summer afternoon like this can be found in all of the southern cities of France (except Marseille). Yes, an avenue in the shade, terrace cafés where beer is drunk. I kept repeating to myself: "Here I am, a greenhorn, a newcomer who is trying so hard to experience Rome as it actually is, that I will perceive nothing." "What are you mumbling about?" — "I'm reciting poetry to myself." — "When you finish you might perhaps try to find a road on your map which takes us to your Bocca di Leone." — "You must admit that's quite a name for a street." — "In Aix-en-Provence there is a Boulevard of Wasted Time; that's not bad either." — "Do you know what the boulevard we're on now is called? Cola di Rienzo. Doesn't that mean anything to you?" — "What *would* mean something to me would be if you'd pay for the beer if you have some change. All I have are these huge 10,000 lira notes."

We drove down the Cola di Rienzo. I sensed that Antoine was entertaining Carthaginian thoughts. He couldn't forgive that roller-coaster, that trap which, in the middle of a desert, plunged us into that maelstrom around the policemen. At every red light he looked right and left at the intersecting avenues and made a face. If he didn't keep repeating "Nîmes, Nîmes" it was because he had a fine sense of subtle differences. Probably he was trying to think of the name of a subprefecture in Auvergne.

Ponte-Margherita. "And then what?" Antoine asked me. — "Then it's straight ahead according to the map." — "Straight ahead is a dead-end, haven't you noticed? There's a wall." It's true, Cola di Rienzo appears to bump into a wall, covered with posters. "They're vile," Antoine added.— "Not really, you're too critical; they're just like any other posters." — "That's exactly what I don't like about them. Furthermore, you must admit that you don't know how to read a map of a city..." — "Well, well, so now Rome is a city! As if we had come here to look for a city!" — "Well, what are we looking for?" asked Antoine. — "What we've been waiting for not only since Civita-Vecchia but since we first started thinking about Rome." I was all wound up and determined to combat my Carthaginian with a bit of eloquence but we had stopped in the middle of a boulevard and someone had been blowing a whistle at us for the last few minutes. It was a policeman, immaculate in white, but with a black glare in our direction. With another of those Roman waves he flagged us in the direction of the wall.

"I'm not stubborn," said Antoine (this meant that he was going to charge like a bull), "if he wants me to bang my head against that wall, O.K., I will."

To be more exact, we would and I thought it was silly. However, two yards from the wall we saw passageways to the right and left. We took the one on the right, emerged and Antoine slammed on the brakes.

After a moment I told him, "This is the Piazza del Popolo." He ignored me completely. Naturally he hadn't parked in a regular parking space—"especially for"— as he called it; he was again a disturber of the peace and the drivers who narrowly missed us made no bones about telling us off. (I had the horrible impression that I understood that kind of Italian right down to the last little subtlety.) Antoine paid no attention to their insolence. He rested his bare arms on the steering wheel and leaned forward to look around.

This was Piazza del Popolo at the moment when the afternoon light has recovered its good humor. I hadn't said a word when Antoine grumbled, "Shut up!" Then he started the car up slowly, leaning as nonchalantly as ever on the the steering wheel. His eyes were not on the road which he was supposed to follow but on the pines of Pincio, Santa-Maria dei Miracoli, Santa-Maria in Montesanto, the Heliopolis obelisk, the fountains. He had taken over the Piazza del Popolo as if it were a family property.

I found it now even easier to understand the vehement Italian of the drivers of cars, buses, carriages and motor-scooters (there were no policemen) — all the more so since we were driving around the square in the wrong direction. Antoine was oblivious because he was engrossed in other matters. Meanwhile, I was making the same remarkable progress in physiognomy that I had made in linguistics and could read, like an open book, the thoughts of the people eating ices on the terrace of the café at the entrance to "Via del Babuino." (There were three or four women among them in front of whom one would not wish to appear ridiculous, even for a kingdom.)

We were now on our fourth trip against the current, our fourth trip before the stares of those three or four "beautiful creatures" and Antoine chose that moment to say rapturously, "It's perfect, old man!" and to give me a whack on the thigh.

One night we were returning home after dinner on the Piazza Navona. We had become Romans from Rome. We didn't go to the tourists' *albergo* ; we frequented a *trattoria* where we were known. (In such a case, one says, "a little *trattoria*".) They always saved a bowl of those little green figs that are eaten with Parma ham and on this occasion had prepared an ox-tail especially for us. There could be no question about its being "especially for us" : we ate it at the owner's table and with the owner's wife. Naturally we felt very smug about this.

"Now let's see if we're going to get lost as we did the last time," said Antoine.

This was said in a very matter-of-fact manner: after the ox-tail and the owner's table, we hadn't a trace of an inferiority complex between us.

I replied, "We have simply to turn after the Borghese palace."

"That's what you said the other night and we ended up like fools at the Pantheon."

"We turned left when we should have turned right."

"I couldn't care less," said Antoine, untruthfully. "I love to get lost in these streets."

We meandered through scenery "à la Piranèse": gigantic baroque shields with standards, pikes, helmets and tapestries of stone faded into the shadows over our heads, and over them hung flying-bridges and vaults which perhaps did not exist (in what we saw it is hard to determine how much was imagination). The streets (alleys without sidewalks comparable to the corridors in Anne Radcliffe's Gothic tales) wind between enormous architectural monuments, the smallest of which would be the pride and joy of an ordinary capital. Naked, raw monuments, moreover, and just as they were when used for various purposes by the Medicis, Madame Marguerite of Austria, Saint Agnes, the Borgias or even Augustus. The streets were illuminated only by dim lights, but they were placed with an extraordinary theatrical sense, and from time to time, after a long, barren wall, between two caryatid gateways, or just beside the palace of the famous poisoner, these streets were studded with small *trattoria* where a few motionless but very much alive Romans were drinking wine.

We were just a few steps from Piazza de Venezia in the heart of Rome, in the section between the Corso and Via Vittorio Emanuele, hardly a bohemian quarter. "The Trastevere where we were the other night," said Antoine, "was pretty much like this but a little more pompous."

"You mean a little less! The Piazza in Piscinula or around Santa Cecilia, at any rate the Via dei Genovesi — that's the stage setting for the Italian comedy; here it's cardinal tragedy; it's a bit loud."

"You don't know what you're talking about," said Antoine. "You're letting yourself be carried away by those tassled hats. Besides, cardinals are never loud; you should learn that once and for all, old man, it will help you get along in life. On the contrary, what was loud the other night was Piazza San Cosimato."

"There wasn't a bit of noise."

"Where did you go to school, kid?" Antoine asked. "Who's talking about noise. I'm talking about a huge façade, low but rose-colored with just the right touch of lime added to it; above it the gray steeple of Santa-Maria in Trastevere and the square unfurling around it. Do you see anything unfurling around here?"

"If you want something that unfurls, let's return to Tivoli."

"It doesn't unfurl at Tivoli," said Antoine. "It unrolls, except, of course, for the view of the *Campagna Romana,* but Tivoli itself is a tapestry; it unrolls."

"You weren't so stingy with words the other morning."

"I'm not stingy tonight," said Antoine, "I'm classifying: in one group the stone (Villa Adriana, for example) in the other, fabrics, — woven goods — if you prefer — the mixtures. A tapestry of pines, cypress trees, fountains and pools. Do you call that being stingy?"

"Let's say that the word was stronger than I intended. Besides, I admit that it isn't the word I was looking for. Anyway, I like you better when you get excited, when you snarl up traffic in the Corso because you have just caught a glimpse of the Trinità dei Monti stairway from the far end of the Via Condotti. The way you drove against traffic with the authority of a Gaul in the midst of all those Romans overjoyed me."

"That was when I first arrived," explained Antoine. "Since then I have sat, like you, as a little Roman from Rome, in the Barcaccia fountain and have looked at the Spanish steps for hours on end."

"Well, in any case, there's one thing we're very much in agreement on: that's in the outward manifestations of our satisfaction. At the peak of your enthusiasm all you can say is: "It's perfect, old man!"".

"Because I'm well behaved," said Antoine. "*You* don't say anything."

"But I share my pleasures with you. Remember the storm over the Capitoline? I could have told you about my rheumatism. We watched in comfort an extraordinary temple of clouds with the Santa Maria in Aracoeli stairway climbing up to it."

"I preferred that storm over the Forum," replied Antoine. "That was the reflection of History."

"By the way," he adds, "we haven't spoken Latin even once."

"You don't know Latin and neither do I."

No, but everyone knows little snatches like *"si vis pace para bellum"*. After all, we all took Latin in college.

"Well," he asked after a pause, "have you located that famous Borghèse palace of yours or are we lost again?"

Hail, sleepwalker ! As we begin our walk let us stop for a moment before this Dioscure of the Capitoline, before this standing dreamer, before this chalky, muscular moon-ghost. Elsewhere it is usually the present which wins out. In Rome, in spite of the bustling streets, in spite of the automobiles, the past often takes its revenge. It pulls itself up to the surface with all the strength of its big marble arms, it emerges in the present and triumphs. With just a little imagination, everything else fades away. There remain only these sleepwalkers, this race of statues on the march.

IN this day and age we have lost the art of traveling, traveling as it was done in the past; that is, to see everything which shows on the surface of cities and people and also to delve thoroughly into the way of life of their inhabitants, to learn their habits and customs, to take part in their life, to find pleasure in their company. This is what President de Brosses and Stendhal did when they went to Italy, when they settled down in Rome for six months or a year. Nowadays we race, we fly; the automobile which brought us quickly carries us to more distant places. No sooner have we arrived than we wish to set off again after a quick look at three or four monuments. No sooner has the plane set us down than we wish to be elsewhere, caught up in the whirlwind of speed: since it took only three hours to come from Paris it shouldn't take more than three days to see Rome.

Alas, in three days the only impression one can have is that of having seen nothing. I remember my frustration during my first, much too rapid trips to Rome. It was as if I had pushed aside a curtain and stolen a glance at a large ballroom during a reception. The little I had been able to see filled me with excitement but I had seen so little ! On each succeeding trip I rushed to new wonders which I had not yet discovered.

Rome is one of those cities which requires very long visits to know it well.

Rome is not only a city, it is the crucible of the Christian world and the tomb of the pagan world. On Rome's soil twenty-four centuries have left their stratifications of souvenirs. Under certain churches there are several layers of crypts or catacombs and the deeper one goes in exploring

13

these layers the farther back one journeys in the course of centuries.

Rome is first of all a modern city, the capital of Italy with its one and one-half million inhabitants, its crowds, its streets lined with elegant stores, its floods of cars and motor-scooters, all that life today offers in the way of hustle and bustle. A rapid rhythm has come to jostle the peaceful image of Rome of olden days when it was not yet the capital of Italy but only that of the Church.

It is the spiritual capital of Christianity and also the temporal capital of the Church States. This Rome still exists, reduced to the Vatican City which has put itself in step with the modern world, having its radio and television stations, its ever-increasing throng of pilgrims. However, papal Rome is not only the Vatican City, it is also the Rome of venerable basilicas which date from the first Christian centuries—San-Giovanni-in-Laterano, San-Paolo-fuori-le-Mura—the Rome of countless churches: "As many churches as there are days in the year", the Rome of catacombs, the Rome of convents and religious communities.

This ancient Rome is still there, imbedded in the new city. And also imbedded there is the antique Rome, pagan Rome with its ruins and columns, its forums and Colosseum, its baths and its palaces on Palatine hill. All that is mixed in with daily life or miraculously isolated in a zone of silence and peace in the middle of gardens, on hilltops, with small streets climbing between long walls above which wave the branches of an oak or a pine.

A museum city, a relic city, a tomb city and also a city full of vitality and jubilation. A versatile city with sections of widely varying atmospheres and with much more striking local colors than those which put Montmartre in contrast with the Latin Quarter.

Before setting out in search of the Rome of

In this dream of stone, in this labyrinth of streets as winding as in a nightmare, not having the means of flying from roof to roof like the quadriga on the preceding page, little Tom Thumb gets lost. Even the Tiber, because of its meandering path, is not a very sure guide. The cars, luckily, have their guardians clothed in candid integrity and white uniforms. "The first street on your right, of course"... The gesture is full of grace.

The Forum's heavy-browed cornice frowns sternly. Is this because it no longer recognizes Rome of the Caesars in this New Yorkish canyon of the Corso? Between the tall cliffs of the palazzi, the automobiles form a sonorous column which fortunately does not trouble the Roman's serenity. On the extreme right, each window shows a different state of the siesta. Opposite, at the entrance to the Corso in the narrow, tightly sealed loggia is total siesta — or who knows what other secret. It was here in this palace that Lætitia Bonaparte died fifteen years after her son. The mother of the Emperor — the one who said, "If only it lasts", and who died in the eternal city.

olden times, let us acquaint ourselves with the Rome of today. We have arrived by car through the Popolo gateway, like Rabelais, President de Brosses, Stendhal, like all the travelers of former times who came on horseback, by carriage or by coach. It was through the Popolo gateway that Charles VIII made his entrance into Rome at the head of a magnificent army which marched from three o'clock in the afternoon until nine at night.

Three streets open off the Piazza del Popolo. Let us take the one in the middle, the Corso, which is Rome's main street, its avenue, the fashionable street. It leads to the Piazza Venezia. Its name comes from the races which formerly took place here, races in which horses were turned loose without harness or rider. The people urged them on with shouts and the winner was awarded a piece of brocade with which it would then strut prancingly through the streets.

Also on the Corso were held masquerades, parades of carnival floats and, during President de Brosses' visits, the promenades "in two endless files of carriages touching each other." Between these two files was an empty lane which only princes could use.

Nowadays the carriages are gone and ordinary mortels have the same rights as princes; they can pass other cars when they feel like it or, at least, when it is possible to do so.

The Corso has remained the center of modern life as it was in the time of the Romans when Via Flamina was lined with colonnades and statues, mausoleums and obelisks which have given way to palaces alternating with places of business, private dwellings and churches. The churches here are often very old but all have been more or less adapted to baroque tastes.

Piazza Colonna with its Marcus Aurelius column opens on the Corso. By Via del Tritone

First appearance, first irruption of a Roman obsession : water. An obsession of a country where the sun overwhelms, where thirst torments, where coolness is a form of paradise. Obsessions, as we all know, lead to madness. At Tivoli the water has gone mad, raving mad, gushing and foaming, dancing with happiness and climbing trees as if drunk with itself. In front of a calm mirror a contemporary lady meditates on her reflection. Seeing such furious gushing, the ancient ladies overhead, overcome by this inebriation, have wrapped one leg around the other.

20

we can go to the Piazza Barberini; by a network of small streets we can reach the stock exchange, the Pantheon, the Minerva temple. We are in the heart of ancient Rome and, at the same time, of present-day Rome. Let us, for this first encounter, allow ourselves be carried along by the crowd to Piazza Venezia, an ideal turn-table for tourists: the best rubs shoulders with the worst; Venezia palace and its balcony from which Mussolini harangued the crowd and the Victor-Emmanuel monument, that cumbersome cake decoration which blocks the view of the Capitol.

If we take Corso Victor-Emmanuel we will find, as on the ancient Corso, the same abundance of churches and palaces interspersed with modern buildings. Rome as Chateaubriand knew it was made up of huts huddled at the feet of tottering palaces. "It appears to be the birthplace of death," he wrote. "There are more tombs than there are dead men. It seems that during the night the skeletons pass from one coffin to another." But life has reclaimed Rome, the dead remain in their coffins, the huts have been replaced by seven storey buildings, the palaces have been restored and the areas surrounding ruins cleared. After the Gesu, a perfect example of the Jesuit-style church, we see on a small square the remains of four temples dating from the Republican era, rediscovered about thirty years ago and which now stand obediently in place, surrounded by trees and shrubbery. Here is a pleasant little square for the pleasure of Rome and then once again churches and palaces, the Chiesa Nuova and the palace of the Chancellery. But perhaps you would rather stop in front of store windows to admire the elegance of Roman blouses and shoes? You're entirely right. For this first day, let's stroll and then sit down at a terrace café before going to dinner at Alfredo's or the Cisterna.

Our tour of Rome should begin with the

Here are our sleepwalkers again. Perched on San Giovanni in Laterano they harangue, declaim, bless, salute, and withdraw. Awakened, the little boy goes off but it would seem that something in those great voices reaches his ears. He turns around and listens. Are the orators attempting to detain him longer on the road to Heaven knows what adventure?

T*he Capitoline is the smallest of Rome's seven hills. It is, however, one of the high spots of our civilization and it seems to be aware of this. This modest hill has calm, self-assured grandeur. It is imposing and knows it. Impassive under a busby of old stones, two columns in the shade of evening stand watch over the welfare of the Empire.*

Forum which was the heart of ancient Rome and which later became Campo Vaccino, such as it was painted in the eighteenth century by Nicole and Hubert Robert, when cattle fed upon grass growing between broken capitals and columns lying on the ground. Here and there a triumphal arch, a few standing columns, a temple transformed into a church during the first centuries of Christianity. Such was the Forum still when Chateaubriand and Stendhal lived in Rome. It was only after 1870 that methodical excavations were undertaken and only in the last fifty years that the Forum has acquired its present-day aspect.

It should be entered with great respect, with a certain fervor, to try to reassemble our memories of Roman history from the first inhabitants who settled on the hills of the ancient city: Etruscans on the Caelian, a Sabine colony on the Capitoline, Latins on the Palatine, without counting the colony of shepherds who had come from the Alban Mountains.

It can be seen that Rome was very early a cosmopolitan city; it was already large when Servius enclosed the seven hills within a fortified wall, of which a few sections are still standing, which probably date from the sixth century B.C.

Here before us is Capitoline Hill which was, as it has so often been drummed into us, near the Tarpeian Rock; it is this small hill which overlooks the Forum. It was crowned with the citadel and the temple of Jupiter the Very Good, Jupiter the Very Great, the oldest and most respected of Roman sanctuaries.

Let us go down into the Forum, originally a foul swamp but since then drained by a canal which was called the Cloaca Maxima; still in existence it can be seen today as it empties into the Tiber just opposite Santa-Maria-in-Cosmedin.

Second irruption of the aquatic obsession: fountains. Fountains everywhere whose cooing trickles into the noises of the s.
bath. And all the stages of the obsession: the thirsty one who strains his neck in vain; the one who drinks his fill; th
one who has sated her thirst and now dreams. Not to mention the Piazza Farnese fountain too high and inaccessible, a l

Water with all its refreshing myths: the fish, the turtle, the
who rolls and laughs under a stream of water; and finally the
cactus whose murmur cools the French ambassador in his office.

Here is something more interesting: the supposed tomb of Romulus. We all know the story of Remus and Romulus suckled by a scrawny, snarling and aggressive she-wolf, now the emblem of Rome which was worshipped on the Capitoline where it may still be seen. Stoop down here: under the pavement of gray stone in front of the Septimius Severus arch, at the spot where a consecrated place seemed to be marked by black marble paving stone, two pedestals were found which formerly must have held two lions and, between them, an enormous block of volcanic tuff and a square stele covered with inscriptions. It is the oldest monument in the Latin language. Recent excavations have also turned up a basin and a bowl dating from the fifth century B.C.

The other monuments to be seen in the Forum, burned by the Gauls, then by Nero and others, date only from the Rome of the Caesars. But how many memories float around each column! In the pale light dancing like golden dust are the silhouettes of the emperors, consuls, tribunes and prefects who held the control of the world within their hands. These nine white columns forming an angle are the portico of the Dii Consentes which enclosed the twelve paired statues of the principal divinities; these three tall, fluted columns are all that remain of the six-columned portico of the Vespasian temple, whereas only the platform remains of the Concord temple. The Septimius Severus arch is complete with its three archways, its columns, bas-reliefs and worn stones but it is unrestored and just as it was built in 203 by the Senate and the Roman populace in honor of the emperor and his sons, Caracalla and Geta, in memory of their victories over the Parthians, the Arabs and the Adiabenians.

Every stone here and even those furrowed by the chariot wheels in the street which crosses the Forum are brilliant with sparkling souvenirs of

Pompous sentinels mount guard before Sant'Angelo Castel. It is a tragic place — tomb, prison, fortress. Under the weight of these memories, under the burden of this enormous mass, the earth seems to give way and the bridge to slide into an abyss. The cyclist sensed this. There is not a minute to lose.

triumphs and victories. Here is the Curia where the Senate met, the Aemilia basilica, the Rostra with sculptured balustrades of the Plutei of Trajan mobile ramparts, the Julian basilica built by Julius Caesar, the eight Ionian columns of the Saturn temple, the altar and podium of the Julius Caesar temple. It was here that his body was burned, that Marc Antony read his will. One is charmed by the elegance of the three Corinthian columns of the Castor and Pollux temple, one of the most graceful evocations of the Forum with the fountain consecrated to Juturna at which the Dioscuri watered their horses after having brought back the news of the Lake Regillus victory. Let us pay a visit to the vestals whose temple and house are found nearby. Their garden welcomes us with its flowers, fountains, its time worn statues of vestals and the foundation of each of the walls.

As we leave pagan Rome for Christian Rome we find one of the most moving edifices it is possible to see—the Santa-Maria-Antiqua church built within older buildings in the fifth or sixth century. These walls lying in ruin are covered with frescoes which have grown dimmer since they were discovered fifty years ago. Certain of them date from the seventh century, other more recent ones from the tenth, and in places there are as many as four layers on top of each other. This church undoubtedly belonged to a Greek monastery. The frescoes are the work of Oriental artists fleeing the iconoclasts' persecutions. The Greek inscriptions give evidence of this as well as the glorification of saints particularly honored in Byzantium like Saint Abacyrus, Saint Sergey, Saint Bacchus, Saint Julitta, Saint Cyriac, etc. Moreover, the style is a mixture of classicism and Byzantine. Admire in particular this tilting angel's head, so grave, so touching.

On the other side of the Sacred Way, two admir-

Only precarious governments, only uncertain religions destroy the signs, symbols and monuments of those who preceded them. Confident in itself, confident in eternity, the Church has neglected to destroy these pagan columns, those of the Faustina Temple. It teaches an important lesson. All glory belongs to God.

The Roman street. Narrow, closed in, without sidewalks. In Paris and London one has the impression that the streets came first and the houses after. In Rome one feels that the street came afterwards, that it was obliged to make its way among the houses. Boys and girls in separate groups. Household chores in permanent view : sweeping and washing. With so much care the wooden fence on the Gianicolo shines like a new penny.

able temples have remained standing which conversion to Christian purposes saved from ruin: the Antonius and the Fausta dedicated by the Senate in A.D. 141 to the memory of the Empress Fausta and, after the death of Antonius Pius, to the worship of his memory. It was transformed into the San-Lorenzo-in-Miranda church and, unfortunately, dressed up in a baroque façade. But its monolithic columns of crystaline marble still sustain a portion of the former entablature and the cella has kept its beautiful frieze of griffins, vases and candelabras.

Beside it the small Romulus Maxentius temple, dedicated in 309 to Romulus, son of Maxentius, is a circular edifice flanked by two attached pavilions. What miracle preserved this Roman monument intact with its bronze door between two porphyry columns?

The three immense brick arches which we see now belong to the Constantine basilica begun by Maxentius; it is one of ancient Rome's most grandiose ruins. They have kept their coffered ceilings. Concerts are still given here.

The arch of Titus is the final element in the Forum. It has only one arcade and was built in A.D. 81 in memory of the victories won by Titus and Vespasian during the Judean War.

Let us now go up to the top of Palatine Hill. From there we will have an over-all view of the Forum. A magnificent view of all the columns, triumphal arches, of those sections of famous walls whose white stones stand in green grass, with the Capitol on one side and the Colosseum on the other.

During the time of the Republic, the Palatine was the elegant section of Rome: it was here that Cicero and Catiline lived and then it was invaded by imperial constructions. When the emperors settled in Byzantium they took with them the most

In the depths of dreams there is anguish. Rome is like a dream. When night has at last emptied the streets, when the human swarm which transforms Rome, as light can transform a room, has disappeared there is something akin to anguish which prowls, which creeps, which steals along these thick walls. It is an intangible anguish which comes out of the ages, made up of memories, of all those presences which are no more, of those dead who are not really dead. These ornate façades seem to hide mysterious dramas within. These windowless walls smother sighs. The past is here, forcing itself upon you, taking you by the throat.

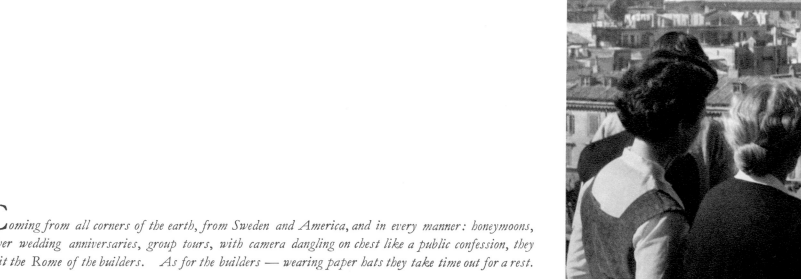

Coming from all corners of the earth, from Sweden and America, and in every manner: honeymoons, silver wedding anniversaries, group tours, with camera dangling on chest like a public confession, they visit the Rome of the builders. As for the builders — wearing paper hats they take time out for a rest.

precious parts of the palaces. In the Middle Ages Italian barons built fortresses on the ruins; in particular, the Frangipani and, during the Renaissance, the Farnese built a splendid villa there surrounded by beautiful gardens. They began to excavate in search of statues but paid no heed to the buildings themselves. It is only in our time that a little order has been put into that chaos.

The Palatinian ruins are less spectacular than those of the Forum, less glorious but perhaps more moving: large porticos, rooms where we see the substructure and remnants of decoration. The Tiberius palace was here, there the Flavian palace furnished by Domitian. And here is the House of Livia which was later taken over by Augustus.

The most impressive building on the Palatine is the Stadium which was also the hippodrome, and the most touching is Romulus' house, remains of huts going back to the early days of Rome—the ninth or eighth century B.C. Thus, with its pines, its shrubbery, its mixture of gardens and vacant ground leaving us the hope of new discoveries, the Palatine is a land of dreams and memories. If we were to come here with a history of Rome in hand, every stone would speak to us of Nero and Caligula, Tiberius and Septimius Severus.

After the palaces of the Caesars we shall now visit the imperial forums. Starting at the Piazza Venezia they present themselves, one after the other, separated from the Roman Forum by one of those large avenues which Mussolini unfortunately had built across ancient Rome.

The Romans had a sense of urbanism. Each emperor wanted to have his forum : a large, monumental square surrounded by public buildings. Julius Caesar set the example by building the Julian basilica. During the Middle Ages and Renaissance it was ravaged and pillaged; every-

Rome is, above all, grandeur. Of course, there is also the gentle side of Rome : the narrow streets, the gardens, Via Appia, evening, the peaceful cloister where a fountain whispers. One may be touched. One may dream. But grandeur soon returns to the fore. Grandeur and strength. A strength which never speaks in a loud voice but which is heard, nonetheless. Rome never lets us forget for long that she was the capital of the world, the capital of strength. Under its gentleness there is a marble fist. The proportions of these columns are so graceful that they appear to be made to the exact measure of man. This is only a courtesy. Look at man there, underneath in the shadow. Beside these columns he scarcely exists, the trail he leaves behind him on earth is scarcely visible. Harum-scarum little man. Rome is also a giant who hides his strength under a mantle of grace.

thing possible was removed and then common dwellings were built in the midst of the ruins. Today, these houses have been demolished and the area around the antique remains cleared.

The first forum we encounter, between two baroque churches, is the Trajan forum, the most beautiful of all with its famous column still almost intact, perhaps the most magnificent in Rome. It is decorated with bas-reliefs describing in a precise manner the expeditions led by Trajan against the Dacians. A stairway inside leads up to the Doric capital where Sixtus the Fifth replaced the statue of Trajan by one of Saint Peter as if it were the apostle who had won the emperor's victories.

The Trajan markets come next, a grandiose, two-storied hemicycle, and then the ruins of the Julian forum and the Venus Genitrix temple of which three columns have been raised again. A little farther on, the forum of Augustus, surrounded by an imposing wall of great blocks of volcanic tuff, has kept several columns of the Temple of Mars Ultor and in the chapel of the Colossus are a few fragments of the hands and a print of the feet of a statue of Augustus, seven times natural size. In the forum of Domitian, completed by Nerva, there remains of the Minerva portico the Colonnace, two enormous Corinthian columns framing a frieze which depicts Minerva teaching mortals the art of weaving, and presiding over the assembly of the Muses.

Changing eras, for in Rome we can pass easily from one to another, we see the Corte porticala transformed in the twelfth century into a lodge for the knights of Rhodes.

Another change of scene: let us cross the street and enter the San-Cosma-e-San-Domiano church. We already noticed from the Roman forum the back part of the temple of the divine Romulus; this time it is the sixth century church which dazzles us with its mosaics. Every man

A strange confrontation, here are two forms of fame : the Pantheon, tomb of Italian kings, and publicity, where the ephemeral goddesses of contemporary life reign. Stone temple and paper castle. Marble column and ad-plastered wall — the eternal and the precarious. Equally indifferent to both, the knife and scissor grinder tours Italy on the spot in the midst of screeching knives. Perhaps he is dreaming of another glory : that of Bartoli.

Sant' Angelo Castel again. Moored to the bank of the river, it takes on the air of an ocean liner guided by its guardian angel captain. As for the column, it is a column. Oh, the magic of a column! It is, perhaps, the most perfect object there is, the object which needs nothing else. A column is enough to fill up a landscape, to animate a ruin. And yet it is only an element. It is easily forgotten. The column is a mysterious unity, perfect and sufficient unto itself.

finds in Rome something to satisfy his taste in art. I confess that I have a penchant for the monuments of the first christian centuries and, in particular, the magnificent mosaics which decorate Rome's oldest churches.

It is an extremely symbolistic art. On the semi-dome of the San-Cosma-e-San-Damiano apse twelve lambs go towards the Divine Lamb while, on a deep blue canopy, Christ stands with hand raised, draped and haloed in gold between Saint Peter, Saint Paul, Saint Theodore and Pope Felix IV.

After visiting this sanctuary we shall go to see the most famous and imposing of Roman monuments, the Colosseum. Although it has served for centuries as a stone quarry, we are always astounded by the majesty of its proportions. In Rome games were as well liked as war. The Colosseum, begun by Vespasian and dedicated by Titus who gave games there for one hundred days in succession, combines the arcade with Greek orders. On the exterior a Doric order is surmounted by an Ionic and then a Corinthian which in turn is surmounted by Corinthian pilasters which support the framework. Between the pilasters consoles pierced with holes sustain masts to which were attached the ropes which supported an immense awning to shade the seats.

All of Roman society with its strict hierarchy would assemble here. Two loges faced each other on the small axis of the ellipse; one was reserved for the emperor, the other for the magistrates. The seats on the first platform were for the senators and vestals, the bleachers on the second floor for the knights, those on the third for the bourgeoisie, while the lower classes sat on the top platform and the women on a platform between the third and fourth level of bleachers.

And now imagine the circus games, the com-

Located on the site of the Domitian stadium, Piazza Navona has kept something of its curious origins. It is vast and airy and as sonorous as a marine shell. Formerly it was flooded for sporting events. The façade of Sant' Agnese glitters in the sky like fireworks. And, to complete the resemblance, a horse and a lion, circus animals, decorate the large Bernini fountain in the center and emerge from stalactite curtains.

The Church, too, has its recreations.   Dressed in white or black — one group obviously
Italian, the other apparently from a colder nation — the same joy prevails in front of the three
chapels, Santa Sylvia, San Andrea and Santa Barbara — or even in the San'Onofrio cloister.

bats of the beast-fighters and wild animals, the gladiators, the martyrs turned over to the wild animals. A whole literature and numerous films have familiarized you with this setting. Don't imitate the Englishman described by Stendhal who entered the Colosseum on horseback coming straight from England and, on seeing a hundred masons at work repairing a wall, exclaimed, "I say! The Colosseum is the best thing I've seen in Rome. This building appeals to me, it will be magnificent when it's finished."

The Constantine arch which is near the Colosseum commemorates, with the battle of Milvio Bridge, the victory of Christianity. Its proportions are admirable but the sculpturing only mediocre; it is an art of decadence. The bas-reliefs and medallions, which are in a very different class, were taken from older monuments.

Upsetting the usual itinerary, let us go to see the antique monuments where they stand. The thermae were not only baths but also casinos and places for reunions and amusements. There were six in Rome, built by Nero, Titus, Trajan, Caracalla, Diocletian and Constantine. Only the Diocletian and Caracalla baths still display imposing ruins.

The Diocletian baths on Viminal Hill were the largest; they contained more than two thousand marble seats for the bathers. Their solid brick walls may still be seen near the station. The main room, the tepidarium, was transformed into a church by Michelangelo, the Santa Maria-degli-Angeli church. Another section became a Carthusian convent and it is now a museum for antiques. It should be visited for it contains an amazing number of masterpieces of ancient sculpture.

The Caracalla thermae, no less gigantic, surpass all the others by their magnificence. They were composed of palaestrae, a stadium, libraries,

A marvel of professional zeal! Even in this place where the frontier between the Vatican and Italy is completely invisible, where there is no barrier, where cars need as a permit only the reflection of the façade of Saint Peter's and its colonnades, the police still watch over their flock with the stern eye of customs officials.

art museums, rooms for resting and conversation. Even deprived of their marble decorations and works of art, these thermae give us an impression of luxury and grandeur.

Nineteen aquaducts carried the water through the Roman country-side necessary for the baths and the fountains which decorated the streets and squares: Rome has remained the city of beautiful fountains. Two of the oldest have been conserved but papal Rome has built other magnificent ones which we shall discover on our walks.

One Roman edifice has come down to us almost completely intact thanks to its being transformed into a church: it is the Agrippa Pantheon built in 27 B.C., restored by Domitian and rebuilt by Adrian on a circular plan. It is a round cella preceded by a portico supported by sixteen enormous columns. This unusual front does not astonish us for it has been imitated so often! But what about the cella? No windows, a hole in the middle. The architect came from the East, a land where it seldom rains. The walls have lost their marble which was replaced by stucco and contain seven recesses which held the statues of gods. These recesses are framed by fluted Corinthian columns. An entablature runs along above them, then an attic where recesses in the form of false windows are alternated with marble panels. The cupola is decorated by five rows of caissons.

Compare this cella to our Gothic churches: what a difference in inspiration, in conceptions of life and death! Rome, moreover, has always been hostile to Gothic architecture. In fact, the only church of this style is found next to the Pantheon; it is Santa-Maria-sopra-Minerva church built on the site of a temple to Minerva. Here the Gothic style is out of place and one does not have the same feelings as when standing before Chartres or Notre-Dame de Paris. We must go in to see the

This colossus, Piazza Navona, represents a river. A figure of speech. One speaks of old man river. At first sight there seems to be no rhyme nor reason for this. Why should a river necessarily be an old man? What old man? And yet it is true that one cannot imagine a river any other way than with a beard, with strong thighs and enormous feet, with the poise of a giant accustomed to floating along, rather than overseeing, with a pensive face.

All artists, all creators are vaguely jealous of the Creator par excellence. The novelist tries to instill life in his characters as God instilled life in the first man. And the architect longs for the sublime order of the forest. The column was, perhaps, born of the tree. The interior of San Paolo fuori le Mura evokes the tree trunks of Fontainebleau, the statues of the Barberini palace recall the splintering barks of palm trees.

works of art and, in particular, Michelangelo's *Christ Carrying His Cross*. Originally the Christ was naked; decency is safeguarded now, for he is clothed in bronze.

Other ancient monuments still spring up here and there in contemporary Rome: the Marcellus theater, begun by Caesar and completed by Augustus, with its three supcrimposed rows of colums, the last of which disappeared in the construction of a palace inside. The Portico d'Ottavia, beside it, once had no less than three hundred columns between two arches of which one still remains. The tomb of Augustus was, in the Middle Ages, a fortress of the Colonna family: it has been restored and repaired just as the Ara Pacis Augustae is once more decorated with the bas-reliefs which had been scattered throughout several museums. On the Piazza di Pietra eleven Corinthian columns caught in the wall of the former Customs House seem to have been a part of the temple dedicated in 145 by Antoninus Pius to the memory of Adrian.

On the other side of the Sant'Angelo bridge, a roman bridge decorated with statues which are not Roman but papal—the angels inspired by Bernini's designs—the enormous round mass of Adrian's mausoleum looms before us. The popes made the Sant'Angelo Castel out of it. It is an immense cylindrical tower over which a tumulus was planted with cypress-trees. Several Roman emperors were buried here. Under the popes it became a real dungeon which Pius IV had surrounded with fortifications. A gallery permitted the popes to come from the Vatican to take refuge here in case of great danger.

The section between Sant'Angelo Castel and the Vatican is called the Borgo. It was full of memories and picturesque charm. On the occasion of the last Holy Year someone had the unhappy idea of splitting it wide open; a large, cold avenue

Night has fallen. An expression which, in this case, is worthless. In Rome night does not fall. One could almost say that it rises. It is wide awake, it shines, it sparkles. The torpor of daytime has been dissipated. A breeze reanimates all creatures. In Rome nightfall has the freshness and vivacity of dawn. And the Milizie tower keeps watch.

Another aspect of Rome-the-forest: this ephemeral light bathing the columns, a light which is like that of a clearing in the woods. We are on the threshold of one of the world's vastest clearings — Piazza San Pietro.

without a soul in spite of a few old palaces lining it, now leads to Piazza San Pietro. The same error was made when the squares in front of the cathedrals in France were enlarged.

Saint Peter's is a huge edifice but its proportions are so ideal that its hugeness is not clumsy. Do not expect enthusiastic praise from me: Saint Peter's leaves me cold and so I will refer you to Stendhal who exclaimed: "Nothing in the world is comparable to the interior of Saint Peter's. After a year's stay in Rome I still went there to spend long hours with pleasure." I confess that I prefer the Constantine basilica a thousand times over.

Everything here, inside and out, is grandiose and unbelievably luxurious. Certain monuments are admirable, such as the Pietà by Michelangelo or Innocent VIII's bronze tomb by Pollainolo. Follow the guide: he will point out everything worth seeing and, if you can, go down into the Vatican grottos to see the ancient necropolis which recent excavations turned up. Not only was Saint Peter's tomb discovered but also many funeral chambers, Christian as well as pagan, with their frescoes and decorations.

Do not ask me either to guide you through the palace and museums of the Vatican. You have only to let yourself be carried along by the crowd. A modern entry has been put at its disposition with a double spiral staircase. A continuous flood of tourists files by in front of the thousands of masterpieces which one would like to contemplate in solitude. Naturally, it is the Chambers and Loges of Raphael and the Sistine Chapel which attract the largest number of shuffling feet. But don't miss the admirable Pinturicchio frescoes in the Borgia apartments if you wish to have a real picture of papal society during the Renaissance. Saint Catherine has assumed the features of Lucretia Borgia. Don't ask to see the Raphael frescoes in

This is the Forum or what is called the attic of our civilization. Here we will find, neatly arranged, some of our most precious treasures. Grandiose bric-à-brac where the centuries, one after the other, have dragged their heavy boots. One dreams of the time when all that was intact. One may also dream of the time when all that was despised, considered old stuff and antique clutter, of the time when the Romans, to build their houses, would come to steal, one a stone, another a column's capitol, when goats grazed at the foot of the altars and where, in this now venerated Forum, the cattle market was held.

60

Cardinal Bibbiena's bath: they are of too frivolous a nature.

When you have contemplated all the marvels of this prodigious museum, when you have posted your mail with stamps from the Holy See and have had your picture taken beside a church guard, we can visit the other sections of this same bank of the Tiber, Trastevere and Gianicolo.

Trastevere is a suburb, a popular section which has been affected very little by modern life. There is a type of Trastevere inhabitant and it is said that it is the true Roman type : strapping fellows with solid fists. In the Middle Ages the "Trasteverins" took part in the battles, continual in those days, under the leadership of their barons, the Anguillaras, whose old thirteenth century palace, situated near the Garibaldi bridge, became Dante's home.

Trastevere is the Rome of artisans, of the little people who sit happily on their doorsteps, surrounded by a swarm of noisy children. Poor, dirty huts and also, as everywhere else in Rome, churches: San Crisogono, a baroque edifice built on top of the ancient church which already existed in the fifth century and which excavations brought to light at the same time as the very expressive frescoes which decorated it dating from the eighth and ninth centuries. Further along we will see the small church of San-Benedetto-in-Piscinula with its romanesque bell-tower, and San Giovanni-dei-Genovesi and its lovely fifteenth century cloister. But the two most beautiful Trastevere churches are Santa-Cecilia and Santa-Maria.

Santa-Cecilia is built on the site of the house, which still exists underground, of Saint Cecilia, a noble patrician executed during the Marcus Aurelius persecutions. You will see in the chancel Maderna's famous statue which depicts her as she appeared lying on her side in the coffin; when the

The moment comes when, by seniority, works of art have a right to their ultimate promotion : they become natural. They enter into the landscape and become a part of it, assuming its color. Under the abuse of time (Why abuse? The storm sometimes curses but what about the rain?); let us say rather, under the caress of time this statue has taken on the grained look, the mossy texture, the relaxed nobility of an old oak. But the expression remains. This old oak is inviting and smiling. Art and nature jointly cast their spells.

62

This magnificent ceiling, this giant saucer which makes one's head turn is the cupola of Saint Peter's. Beneath it, overhanging the papal altar is the Bernini tabernacle which is also called the baldachin. The antique column was born of the straight line. Look well at these twisting columns : you will not find an inch of straight line. The straight line has been excluded, exiled. This is because it is the shortest distance between two points and baroque art does not care a bit about getting there fast. These twisting columns are well aware that they must go up. So be it, they go up but strolling along, endlessly seeking an escape, allowing themselves all the diversions of the curved line. Baroque art is art gone mad. Mad about itself. Enchanted with being, charmed by its own spell, running after every butterfly, chortling at its own convolutions. Destination ? What destination could possibly give me the pleasure I find in merely existing ? From this springs superabundance, feverishness, exaggeration — the stuff pleasure is made of.

latter was opened in 1599 the artist was present. He sculptured her with a veil hiding her face, two locks of hair showing, her arms spread out in front of her, hands slightly open and knees half bent, her dress draping a thin, frail body down to her bare feet showing below. She would seem asleep were it not for her severed neck which reminds us that she was beheaded.

The Santa-Cecilia church is charming with an atrium preceding it and in the middle a large basin in which rests a vase formerly used for ablutions. The façade is baroque with a portico, but a Romanesque bell-tower appears above it. From the ancient church, there remains in the chancel reserved for nuns, an admirable and precious masterpiece, a fresco by Pietro Cavallini, that great innovator of the end for the thirteenth century, Giotto's rival. In *The Last Judgment* which we see at Santa-Cecilia's he shows himself to be an original master, using a neo-hellenism of extraordinary nobility, simplicity and sobriety. The stern-faced apostles surrounding Jesus and the angels with grave and gentle feminine faces mark a date in the history of painting.

Too often in Rome the Romanesque churches were demolished or mutilated during the baroque period. Santa-Maria-in-Trastevere, luckily, has remained about as it was when Innocent II had it rebuilt in 1140. Fontana remodeled the portico in 1702 but kept the twelfth and thirteenth century mosaics above it, a series of feminine figures carrying lamps, surrounding the Virgin and the Infant Jesus. Inside there is a magnificent group of mosaics.

The apse portrays Christ and Mary surrounded by saints. The Virgin is dressed as a Byzantine empress while the standing saints, shown full-face, have stocky bodies, round faces and are dressed in loose draperies. These mosaics are certainly the

To what can one compare this crowd under the dark cupola of
night?   To a flower bed?   To a smouldering fire?   Faith is like
a flame.   Reduced to a luminous skeleton, Saint Peter's makes one
forget its grandeur.   Only the delicacy of its lines remains.

work of Roman artists but the style of the composition remains Byzantine.

The six works relating to the life of Mary which complete those on the vault are of later date and are the work of Pietro Cavallini whose *Last Judgment* is in Santa-Cecilia's. When you go to lunch in one of the good restaurants to be found on the square in front of Santa-Maria, be sure to enter the church to admire these mosaics. They are among the things in Rome which must be seen.

Nearby is the Corsini palace which is now an art museum.

Opposite it, the Farnesina villa will give you a most elegant vista of Rome of the Renaissance. The extravagant banker Chigi whose palace we saw on the Corso, had it built by Peruzzi and decorated by the best artists of that time. Raphael painted religious subjects for the Vatican. Here he was dealing with profane themes. Most engaging interpretations of the mythology of the classic poet Politian are to be found in the scenes by Raphael, his students and disciples. Raphael's *Galatea* has a luminous and Vergilian grace about it and his *Fable of Psyche* shows how well the spirit of antiquity flourished again under the reign of Leon X. On the second floor *The Marriage of Alexander and Roxane* by Sodoma possesses that vague and insinuating voluptuousness which is characteristic of that artist's very personal style.

In a neighboring room Peruzzi painted the gods of Olympia and scenes of Rome as it was during Raphael's time. We meet him again at San-Onofrio where he painted, at the same time as Pinturicchio, scenes from Mary's life. Tasso died in the San-Onofrio convent and several rooms have been dedicated to the author of *Jerusalem Delivered*.

Here begins the Gianicolo promenade from which we have an admirable view of the eternal city lying at our feet. One of the great pleasures

Is this only another photograph? Isn't it rather one of those great Renaissance paintings? A painting which might be entitled The Triumph of Religion. *God is, of course, present in the humblest country church. But God is strength too. God is triumph. Faith is found in prayer. It is found also in this fervent affirmation which rises towards the heavens, in this ornate and glorious Jacob's ladder which is strong enough to bear any weight, in this golden allegory of which all the lights, the glitter, the prestige are brought together in this man dressed in white.*

of Rome is to walk in the center of the city or on its outskirts under these oaks and big umbrella pines whose majesty is worthy of the noble buildings which we have just left behind. The Gianicolo promenade leads to the Doria Pamphili villa which Camillo Pamphili, the nephew of Innocent X, had built in 1650 by Algardi.

We will descend by way of the Paola fountain built in 1612 by Fontana and Maderno at the order of Paul V, where we will see once more the six granite columns originating from the portico of the former church of Saint Peter. And on a terrace from which we have another marvelous view of Rome, we see the San-Pietro-in-Montorio church which already existed in the ninth century and was reconstructed at the end of the fifteenth. Among its paintings is the famous *Flagellation* by Sebastiano del Piombo, carried out according to designs by Michelangelo. Admire its vigorous and dramatic character, its painful brutality, and don't miss seeing in the convent's courtyard the famous Tempietto, a small edifice by Bramante which is one of the most perfect works of the early Renaissance.

We have visited the various forums and the Palatine but we have not yet seen the Capitoline; this is the moment to go there. Don't expect to find anything at all—except for the sculptures in the museums—which recalls ancient Rome. The Aracoeli church is located on the site of the Arx, the Caffarelli palace on that of the Jupiter temple, the Senate palace on that of the ancient library. However, thanks to Michelangelo, the Capitoline lives again in an orderly square which is a model of harmony and efficient use of space.

Let us visit the Capitol museum, since in Rome one goes from one museum to another, if only to see *The Dying Gaul, The Thorn Puller, The Faun with Grapes, Venus of the Capitoline, The Drunken Old*

My child, what are you doing there? Aren't you frightened of being caught in that spider's web, lost in a desert whose severity evokes heaven knows what cruel philosophical system? Beware! That almost metaphysical emptiness has already eaten into the statue — and your shadow appears to me to be firmly enmeshed.

P ower in Rome is a decent sort of fellow. The Quirinale, the President of the Republic's residence, is on the same level as the square. Its gentle slope is a narrow, slightly convex oval. The rest is turned over to the children. In Italy the child is king. Just try to scold Junior in the street .you'll start a riot and all those knitting mothers will turn aggressive. Look at this little boy in the Pincio gardens. He has a right to a private performance. Louis XIV in all his glory had nothing better.

Woman, an archaic *Apollo* of the fifth century and *Venus of the Esquiline*, that charming young girl combing her hair.

Reconstructed by the Fransicans, the Santa-Maria-in-Aracoeli church, looming at the top of an interminable stairway, presents an unfinished façade. It was here that the sibyl of Tibur predicted to Augustus, who came to consult her on the choice of a successor, that the birth of a Child of Judea made all such worries superfluous since that Child was to be responsible henceforth for the welfare of the world. He is there, that Child, in a niche under a glass globe, bedecked in jewels and surrounded by lights. Sealed envelopes coming from all corners of the earth lie at His feet. He is brought out of His niche on a small chariot to a group of women who kneel down and make the sign of the cross. The Bambino has replaced the sibyl.

If we follow the Via del Mare which brings us closer to the Tiber, we will find a whole series of monuments which have been isolated and restored, anyone of which would be the pride of a small city: the house of Cescentius, the only example in Rome of a seigniorial dwelling of the Middle Ages largely constructed with Roman fragments; the temple of Fortuna Virile, extremely pure and elegant; the charming Vesta temple with a circular cella, surrounded by twenty Corinthian columns; the arch of Janus Quadrifrons, a massive construction with four large arcades and two rows of niches; the arch of the Argentariorum; the Romanesque church San-Giorgio-in-Velabro with a portico and bell-tower; and, lastly, Santa-Maria-in-Cosmedin, the parish church of the Greeks who took refuge in Rome after fleeing the Oriental persecutions. It is one of the rare churches in this city which has not suffered baroque abuse, one of the most moving and impressive. It is an eighth-

A *moment of inattention and anguish returns. If a place destined to be swarming with people stands empty, anguish sets in immediately. Deserted squares, abandoned arenas, theater wings when the play has ended. And it is of theater wings we think here in this colosseum lying in ruins. Monstrous wings where the papier mâché is turned to stone, where drama froze in is tracks, where the blood which ran was real blood and the agonized cries were not simulated. A place where men met their death — such a place is never appeased. Little anguish, where are you going? What are you carrying in your bag?*

At first glance, the Roman countryside seems harsh and monotonous. For a long time travellers said unkind things about it. Montaigne, for example, saw only an "unpleasant country, uneven and full of crevices... the ground naked and treeless." It took Chateaubriand to discover its charm and majesty. It is true that some painters before him appreciated it, but not without a certain reticence which is the very reticence of this secret country. "We have some letters written by the great landscape painters: Poussin and Claude Lorrain make no mention of the Roman countryside. But if their pens were silent how eloquent were their brushes! The agro romano was a mysterious source of beauty into which they dipped while keeping it secret, out of a sort of genius' avarice and the fear that the vulgar would profane it." (Chateaubriand).

century basilica, slightly modified in the twelfth century, with three naves separated by antique columns, an iconostasis, an ambo with its paschal candles, mosaic décorations and precious marble from the Greek Island of Kos.

As we leave, let us look at the beautiful highly decorated fountain by Bizzaccheri and then turn our steps towards the Aventine. We pass in front of the Maxim circus which was the largest in Rome; it could hold more than 300,000 spectators. It has been repaired recently.

The Aventine, after having been an aristocratic section during the Empire, became a neighborhood of convents during the Middle Ages and so it has remained. The site is peaceful, the landscape gentle. One has a view on the other side of the Tiber of the Janiculum and Vatican hills. The first church which we encounter is Santa-Prisca, built in the fifth century on the ruins of the house of Aquila and Prisca. In the crypt there is a venerated hollow capital which Saint Peter used for baptisms when he lived in this house. Not long ago a chamber for the worship of the Persian god Mithras was discovered in the basement, along with remains of paintings.

Santa-Sabina which we see next is one of the Roman churches I like the best. It was built in 425 on the site of one of those primitive churches, the *tituli*, installed in private homes. It belonged to the matron Sabina. Saint Dominic founded a convent there. Let us first admire the wooden door dating from the first half of the fifth century with its eighteen carved panels representing scenes from the Old and New Testaments. There are three naves inside the church. It is the only fifth century basilica still existing in Rome. We are taken back to the early days of Christianity. The columns which separate the three naves were taken from a pagan temple and the arches are

We return to the Trajan column but from another side where it keeps its distance and all its majesty. The Roman street has the cheerfulness of a circus. It is lively, noisy and animated. One always has the impression that there must be a celebration three blocks away and that everyone is hurrying to it.

decorated with polychrome marble. Of the mosaics which covered the walls only one remains. Let us look, too, at the pretty Romanesque cloister and the orange tree planted by Saint Dominic.

And now we arrive at one of the most delightful places in Rome, the Piazza dei Cavalieri di Malta, created by Piranesi who decorated the Priorato church. Let us stroll in the gardens before going up to San-Saba whose façade is preceded by a Romanesque porch with columns taken from pagan edifices.

We can now go down to the Saint-Paul gateway which has conserved its imposing Roman military appearance, next to which stands the Caius pyramid. It is one of the most famous of Roman views, one which was very dear to travelers of yore but which automobile traffic today prevents us from enjoying to the fullest.

We have only to go straight ahead to arrive at San-Paolo-fuori-le-Mura, the largest church in Rome with the exception of Saint Peter's. It was also the most beautiful one with its collection of frescoes and mosaics until 1823 when a fire destroyed it almost completely. It was restored in the same style but the spell was broken. The cloister, however, deserves close attention. It is almost too lavish with its twin columns, fabulously convoluted and decorated with mosaics. Here, thirteenth century Romanesque art shows extraordinary over-refinement.

In the nearby Commodilla catacombs some of the most beautiful frescoes of Christian Rome have recently been discovered.

Straight ahead is the Tre Fontane Abbey, built on the spot where Saint Paul is believed to have been beheaded. Tradition has it that three fountains sprang up at the three places where his head bounced. Three churches, more or less remodeled

Perhaps nothing can equal the charm of a late afternoon stroll on the Palatino. The past is present here. So closely blended with nature that it becomes amenable and smiling. Nature is here. It borrows the solemnity of the neighboring columns and marble sunk in the ground. Everything is as it should be. Everything is in harmony. The tranquillity of the tree accentuates the serenity of the column.

Huge armored tank immersed in the night, the Colosseum fires away through every loophole.

in the sixteenth century, surrounded by eucalyptus trees stand in this humid, marshy, oasis-like place which is, nonetheless, full of poetry and simplicity.

Let us imitate the pilgrims and drink at each fountain before going to see the other churches outside the walls. And first of all, leaving by the San Lorenzo gateway which replaces the Tibur gateway built by Augustus, here is San-Lorenzo-fuori-le-Mura, one of the most venerable churches in Rome.

It is composed of two churches, one of which was built by Constantine in 330 on the tomb of the martyr; the second, built by Sixtus III around 435, adjoined the other but faced in the opposite direction. In 1216 Honorius III united the two churches and built a bell-tower. The exterior ressembles the usual barn with a portico, the interior is a classical basilica in all its nobility. The change from paganism to Christianity did not, in Rome, bring about a revolution in the art of building: the same serene gravity remained. This edifice is particularly impressive with its raised choir, its mosaics, ambos and pavement from Kos.

The Sant'Agnese-fuori-le-Mura church is one of the most touching. It was built in 324 on the catacombs where the martyr's body had been placed by Constance, daughter of Constantine. Here the Renaissance is wedded with the art of the first centuries, represented by traditional antique columns and a beautiful mosaic dating from 625-638 of purely Byzantine inspiration and famous for the delicacy of its colors. Saint Agnes is depicted as a Byzantine princess dressed in a jewel-covered robe between Pope Honorius I, holding a model of the church in his hand, and Pope Symmachus, both restorers of the basilica.

Nearby the Saint Constance mausoleum, transformed into a baptistery, then into a church, is a strange building, circular in form with a cupola

A museum, the Galleria Borghese, has the coquetry to show us a façade as ornate as a picture. A woman hurries up the stairs. She has a date with Canova, Raphael, Botticelli. The green depths of the Villa Borghese spread out in front of the Gallery. In Rome the gardens' theme replies to the fountains' theme to compose a hymn to refreshing coolness.

Here, helter-skelter, is an Italian film in the best neo-realistic style. Yielding to temptation, Gigetto has stolen a bicycle. Filled with remorse, he takes advantage of his mother's absence (she is at the market) to try to take a train at the Stazione di Termini. The sight of the police stops him. The distraught father goes to implore the Madonna's aid. He meets two priests — in Italian films there are always priests passing by, no one knows just why. But there will be a happy ending : a fruit peddler will take Gigetto in and stuff him full of grapes.

supported by twenty-four granite columns joined in pairs, whereas the encompassing gallery is capped by an annular cradle-vault. The mosaics on this vault are the oldest known Christian mosaics. Their figurines on a white background, their genii, cupids and harvesters recall Roman frescoes. In the small apses later mosaics from the fifth or seventh century, accompanied by a beautiful cornice of fruit, depict the entrusting of the keys and the Redeemer giving peace to the world.

We return to Rome through the Pia gateway built at the time of Pius IV by Michelangelo and, just for the sake of changing periods, we will go to see a few baroque edifices along the way. First of all, the Acqua Felice fountain, fed by an aquaduct, and designed by Fontana. Don't criticize the statue of Moses, poor Prospero da Brescia died of grief from the unkind remarks of his contemporaries. The Santa-Maria-della-Vittoria church, facing the square, contains one the most astonishing examples of baroque decoration with colored marble and brilliant luxuriousness. This should be seen as well as Bernini's *Saint Theresa*, his most famous work. The saint, in one of those tormented attitudes of which Bernini had the secret, swoons, her heart pierced by an arrow shot by divine love.

We re-encounter Bernini in the little church of San-Andrea-al-Quirinale, one of his most original conceptions with an interior in elliptic form and a baldachin-covered porch. Here too, the interior is rich in colored marble.

Close by, the San Carlino church, also baroque, is the first work by Borromini who gave it the proportions and curious form of one of the pillars of Saint Peter's dome.

We have now arrived at the Quattro Fontane crossroads, four intersecting streets with cut corners holding fountains representing Fidelity,

"*Professor Gottling entered: he had returned a short time before from a trip to Italy. I was delighted to see him again and drew him into a window-recess to hear his impressions. 'If you want to become somebody,' he said, 'it is to Rome that you should go! What a city! It is a whole life and a whole world... As soon as we enter Rome a transformation takes place in us and we feel as big as the surroundings.' (Goethe's Conversations with Eckermann).*

Strength, the Arno and the Tiber. It is one of the most typical places in the city, each street having as a perspective the obelisks of the Quirinale, of the Santissima Trinita-dei-Monti, of the Esquiline, and the Pia gateway.

But it is the Quirinale square especially which will give us a picture of that baroque Rome which has kept its sense of grandeur. In the middle of the square loom the Dioscuri, two colossal statues found in the baths of Constantine and, between them, an obelisk coming from the Augustus Mausoleum towers over a basin originating in the Forum. On the north and west are two palaces, the Consulta and the Quirinale, whose façade was done by Bernini. It serves as the residence of the President of the Republic who has succeeded the Italian kings as the latter succeeded the popes.

We are on top of Quirinal hill and the square is barred on the west by a balustrade from which one may look down on the entire center of the city.

On returning to Piazza Venezia we pass between two other palaces: the Rospigliosi—built in 1603 on the site of the Constantine baths, and belonging at one time to Mazarin—and the Villa Colonna palace, famous for its picture gallery.

We have still to see two great basilicas of Rome : Santa-Maria-Maggiore and San-Giovanni-in-Laterano and... a few others.

We will start with San-Pietro-in-Vincoli, the façade of which faces a rectangular square to which a palm tree and a tower of the Middle Ages give character. Empress Eudoxia, wife of Valentinian III, founded this basilica in 455 to hold Saint Peter's chains. It was altered during restorations in the fifteen and eighteenth centuries but has kept its majestic and severe appearance, its three naves separated by twenty antique Doric and fluted columns. At the back of the nave the heirs of

With its bare, pierced façade which is almost coarse, with its square door and unpolished lines, Santa Maria d'Aracœli has the dignified simplicity of a barn. A celestial barn for God's harvest.

Beside this church nested like a bird in the remains of the Baths, San Paolo fuori le Mura, newly rebuilt, looks like a youngster. San Giovanni in Laterano is somewhere in between the two. On the right is Santa Maria in Cosmedin where the Bocca della Verità is located. The latter, according to legend, will bite the hand of a liar. Let us leave it at that, it's safer. But who would dare to tell a lie in this light of the full moon?

Julius II placed his mausoleum on which Michelangelo worked for forty years. It was to be composed of forty statues; here there are only six—three by Raffaele da Montelupo, three by Michelangelo himself. Two are rather mediocre but Moses is a masterpiece which symbolizes very well the unconquerable spirit of the terrible pontiff, Julius II.

Now let us visit San-Martino-ai-Monti, constructed in 1650 by Pietro da Cortona on the former site of a fourth century church with twenty-four antique columns; it contains paintings by Gaspard Poussin and, more important, under the crypt, the remains of the *titulus* Equitii, a church installed in a private home in the fourth century. It is a large, vaulted room divided into two naves by pillars.

The Santa-Prassede church a little farther on, dedicated to one of Pudenziana's daughters who gave shelter to Saint Peter, is mentioned as early as the fifth century. It is a basilica with three naves separated by granite columns and pillars. Here may be seen the well in which Saint Prassede hid the last remains of the martyrs. It also possesses one of the largest groups of mosaics in Rome : commissioned by Pope Pasquale I (817-824) who buried his mother in the San-Zenone chapel, the mosaics cover the apse and the whole interior of the chapel. The latter was called the Garden of Paradise and it can bear comparison with the most celebrated monuments of Ravenna. Its cupola, like those of Byzantine churches, is raised on a square plan. With its pavements of polychrome marble and its Byzantine-inspired mosaics the mausoleum of the pope's mother resembles that of an empress of Constantinople.

As we leave don't miss seeing a good painting by Guilio Romano, *The Flagellation*, and in a recess the column which is said to be that to which Christ was tied for whipping.

Shadow, great yawning shadow. What phantoms lurk in the depths of this opaque night ?

97

From living among statues, one acquires a certain grandiloquence. If he has just missed his bus the Roman easily assumes the convulsed facial expression of the Laocoon, and if he loses his keys he is just as griefstricken as the dying Gaul. Perhaps this priest simply wishes to protect himself from a draft. His gesture is as graceful, or almost, as that of Moses who, behind him, so furiously berates purely mechanical civilization. On the right, beside the fountain whose perfect form is outlined against the sky, three other priests, younger and as yet unjostled by life, represent rather well the three essential activities of the mind : contemplation, meditation, reading.

We have reached the Santa-Maria-Maggiore church, built in the fourth century after an apparition of the Virgin asking that a church be built for her at the place which, the next morning, would be covered with snow. Rebuilt, enlarged and given a baroque façade, it has conserved the imposing appearance of a basilica. The coffered ceiling is by Sangallo and the floor of Kos origination. "It's a drawing room," Stendhal said. A magnificent drawing room and gilded with the first gold brought from Peru. Two chapels are especially sumptuous: the Sistine and the Pauline chapels.

But we are more interested in the mosaics. Several different periods are represented. Those decorating the principal nave, above the entablature and on the triumphal arch, date from 432-440, Sixtus III's pontificate.

It is composed of a series of pictures representing Biblical scenes in which we see Abraham, Jacob, Moses, Joshua at the head of crowds and armies, encouraged by Christ and angels coming out of clouds and making stones rain down on their adversaries. It is a transitory art, still very akin to Roman paintings of the Imperial era but in which one senses already a searching for new aesthetics. Gold backgrounds begin to appear and the unity of space is broken.

On the triumphal arch, as if continuing the Biblical scenes, are several episodes from Evangelical history already denoting a more Oriental character. To the apse which was originally decorated only with scrolls, birds and cupids, Jacopo Torriti added in 1295 a Coronation of the Virgin and various other mosaics.

Since a church was dedicated to Saint Prassede, it was only fair that another be dedicated to her sister, Saint Pudenziana. It, too, dates from the fourth century but has been remodeled several times and a small Romanesque bell-tower added.

An arch and its perfect curve, massive columns, entablements for giants, sun and shadow alternated, a thick, rough stone, stone that fortresses and prisons are made of, a few scenes frozen in the memory, the violent bites of time, a narrow door and beyond it a few shacks : never, perhaps, has there been a more perfect image of glory.

Here also we find in the apse a fourth century mosaic spoiled in part by a sixteenth century restoration. Christ, seated on a magnificent throne, an open book in his hand, is surrounded by the two saints, Prassede and Pudenziana, and by the apostles wearing togas like senators

Now let us go to see San-Giovanni-in-Laterano. It must be admitted that this church is disappointing. It was here that the palace and church of the first popes stood, the land given by Constantine. The church, destroyed by the Vandals and restored by Saint Leon in the fifth century, then by Adrian I in the eighth, destroyed again by an earthquake in 896, was rebuilt in 905 and so well decorated by Nicolas IV that it was considered in the thirteenth century as the most beautiful edifice in the Christian world. But new fires ruined it while the popes were in Avignon and, on their return, they abandonned Laterano for the Vatican. Certainly the basilica was rebuilt in an imposing style, as was the palace, but all those constructions remain lifeless and hardly moving except for the cloister which is still more beautiful and richer than that of San-Paolo-fuori-le-Mura—the most magnificent example of the stone of Kos—and than the San-Giovanni baptistery which dates from Constantine's reign. It was the prototype of all those built since then: eight porphyry columns support eight others on which the cupola rests. Look at the mosaics in the chapels and listen to the bronze door which undoubtedly comes from the Caracalla baths and which the guide will make vibrate gently for you. If you have the courage, go up the Scala-Santa, the stairway taken from Pilate's palace in Jerusalem which Jesus climbed on the day of his passion. It may only be climbed on one's knees.

The Laterano palace has become a museum but when one has seen the museums of the Vatican and

One after the other, the centuries have passed over Rome like alluviums, each one leaving its trace and all these traces superimposed. Here History can be seen in transversal cutting, in its geological layers.

*A*fternoon *is drawing to an end. Heat and business matters are forgotten at the same time. Men and statues enjoy a little moment of happiness — with the same gestures, the same abandon.*

the Capitol, the antiquities sheltered here have little interest; I would suggest instead that you go to the Maggiore gateway where the square has just been lowered two meters to free the base of the baker Eurisace's tomb.

We will now direct our steps towards the Caelian Hill. The first church we encounter is the Ss. Quattro-Coronati which tradition names as the saints Severo, Severiano, Carpoforo and Vittorino. Built in the fourth century, destroyed by the Normans, it was rebuilt in 1111. This time it is not mosaics which we shall find but frescoes.

San-Clemente, a little farther on, is a fascinating edifice. This basilica is one of the oldest in Rome; Saint Jerome already mentions it in 392 but it was destroyed by Robert Guiscard's soldiers when the city was pillaged. In 1108 Pasquale II built a second church on the ruins of the first, using the marble which decorated it. The new basilica was modified during the baroque period and no one remembered the first until it was discovered one hundred years ago and the grounds cleared around it.

Thus we have two churches. The upper is not lacking in interest with its small twelfth century porch, its mosaics of the same period and its tombs but on descending into the lower church one really goes back into the night of history, into the first centuries of Christianity and what one sees is stupendous : the house of Saint Clement himself and a Mithras sanctuary. It is supposed that the saint's house was confiscated and turned over to the priests of Mithras. The ceiling imitates that of a cavern and we see the god on a half-column, wearing his ceremonial headdress and offering a bull in sacrifice.

But let us return to the middle level, the lower church. The walls are decorated with frescoes from different periods, principally the ninth and

Here is that water obsession again. Divine water of Villa d'Este ! Whether it be to keep, to capture, to charm, to honor, to retain by any means possible. A passion which even goes so far as to try to transform water, to make something out of it which can no longer escape, something almost solid, almost edible, so to speak. Foliage, trailing vines, water like whipped cream. The table is set, the buffet is ready.

One must go to the very core of words. In architecture there is archer. In archer there is arch. The archer is invisible. The arch is there, the keystone, so to speak, of Roman architecture. Bridges, aquaducts, basilicas like so many bows shooting all their arrows heavenwards.

eleventh centuries, which are similar to those we saw at Santa-Maria-Antiqua. The most astonishing, perhaps, is an Ascension painted around 850 during the time of Pope Leon IV who had himself portrayed in a corner of the fresco with a rectangular halo. The style is very modern, very expressive and characterized by violent, exaggerated movements. A *Descent into Limbo* of very schematic style and a warmer toned Deification— a painting of the Saints surrounding the Virgin— date from the same period.

We will receive the same kind of impression on visiting the Ss. Giovanni-e-Paolo church, built on top of the house of the two martyred saints in the fourth century. It was largely remodeled in the 12th century but, here too, it is the underground part which is the most interesting. We find ourselves in a two-storey house which is, at the same time, a Roman palace, a Christian home and an oratory as is indicated by the frescoes—pagan in some places with little genii holding garlands, peacocks and birds; Christian in others with the fish, the dove, the pitcher of milk and the lambs. Personages praying as the first Christians did, standing, their arms held out in the form of the cross, blindfolded martyrs waiting to be beheaded, all the atmosphere of the life of the early believers is found in these underground dwellings which even include the bathroom and the cellars with their amphorae.

The Caelian Hill like the Aventine delights us with its shady peace, its small, deserted streets, its aspects of a cloistered city. One may linger to dream in the gardens of the Celimontana villa with its rare and wonderful plants—the palace shelters the Geographical Society—before the Santa-Maria-in-Domnica mosaics, or in the circular church of San-Stefano-Rotondo, a strange fifth century building composed of two circular naves.

We return by way of San-Gregorio-Magno,

Villa Adriana is a souvenir album but a souvenir album for an emperor. For an emperor who had at his disposal far better equipment than a lowly camera. To remember the places which had impressed him the most during his travels — the Prytaneum in Athens, the Canopus temple, the Vale of Tempe — Adrian had them reproduced and reconstituted here. Even in the midst of ruins, something of his intention remains and especially at sunset Villa Adriana has the tender and melancholy sweetness of memory.

rebuilt during the baroque period and famous for its paintings by Guido and Domenichino. Poussin said of the latter: " He is first after Raphael." All during his lifetime Domenichino was attacked by his enemies, his rivals, who could not forgive him for his talent and at last succeeded in poisoning him. He knows how to be dramatic : admire his *The Martyr of Saint Andrew*. He also knows how to be gentle and tender as shown in his frescoes dedicated to Saint Cecilia in the San-Luigi-dei-Francesi church.

That is still another church which must be seen, one of those which we are going to visit during a last walk through Rome across this section swarming with life situated between the Tiber and Piazza Venezia which we have not yet explored. It is the best known section too, the richest in palaces of the Renaissance or seventeenth century and in baroque churches.

San Luigi-dei-Francesi which dates from the Renaissance is famous for its paintings: those of Domenichino and Caravaggio's two masterpieces: *Vocation* and *The Martyr of Saint Matthew*.

At Saint-Agostino, another Renaissance church, we will see Raphael's *The Prophet Isaiah* and Jacopo Sansovino's *Madonna del Parto ;* at Santa-Maria-della-Pace the celebrated *Sibyle* by Raphael and the cloister by Bramante; in the crypt of Santa Agnese-in-Agone the bas-relief depicting the saint about to submit to torture, covered by her hair. We already know that the church was built on the ruins of the Circo Agonale where the saint was exposed naked. Luckily, her long hair hid her from the lustful eyes of the pagans. The church's façade, of pure baroque style, is by Borromini; the three fountains on the Piazza Navona, which has conserved the form of the Circo Agonale, are due to Bernini's inspiration. It is the most astounding baroque group imaginable with its extremely mus-

A man is talking on the telephone. Only the sculptured heads listen to him. He personally does not appear to listen very attentively to what is being said. He looks at the girl. The girl looks at her mother. The fiancé looks at the photographer. All these good intentions which never get together.

Churches : San Vincenzo e San Anastasio, La Sapienza, Santa Maria della Pace, Santa Maria in Trastevere, churches everywhere like a vigilant army. Of every age, of every form—round or square, convex or concave. And columns like so many streams in a fountain, motionless, frozen in their upward thrust but remaining mysteriously alive.

cular statues of river tritons, fat-cheeked from blowing in conchs, the animals, the Ethiopian wrestling with a dolphin; a great outburst of forms in action, treated with a sort of fury by the pupils of Bernini.

As for the palaces, the most beautiful is the one occupied by the French Embassy, the Farnese Palace, begun by Antonio Sangallo and completed by Michelangelo. The façade is sober and imposing, the courtyard magnificently arranged with its three rows of large arcades. Be sure to see the gallery where Annibale Carracci painted, on a background of colossal forms and sham architecture, mythological scenes full of voluptuousness. It was here that Le Brun found the model for his famous galleries.

The Spada palace next to it with its courtyard and richly decorated façade; the Madama palace, former palace of the Medicis now occupied by the Senate; the Montecitorio palace begun by Bernini which now houses the Chamber of Deputies; the Borghese palace; the Lancelotti; the Turci—there are a hundred palaces, classic or baroque, which catch the eye, which have a story to tell us or dark secrets to reveal.

It is not a month that one should spend in Rome, it is a year, a whole lifetime. And we haven't yet seen the Tritone fountain nor, more important still, the Trevi fountain. Let us run to throw a few lire in it to be sure of coming back someday. It is the proudest, most monumental of Rome's fountains just as the Piazza di Spagna is the most evocative, the most unforgettable of all the Eternal City's squares. Above the Barcaccia fountain, designed by the father of Bernini, and the flower sellers' displays, the stairway springs up, straight at first and then in elliptic form before joining the Trinità-dei-Monti church built at the expense of Charles VIII of France just as the stair-

We have already met one of the Dioscuri. Was it Castor or Pollux? Nobody knows for they cannot be told apart. Here are both of them, watching over the Capitoline together. They have dismounted, peaceful conquerors, armed only with their presence, advance guard of an army which is consulting together behind them. One facing the sun and the other with his head slightly turned, each is a picture of calm. Who could disturb them? What explosion, what cataclysm? Undoubtedly nothing. They are settled in this magic instant where there is neither past nor future, where nothing more can happen. Castor and Pollux are soon to be carried into the heavens where they will become stars. A good reason to arm oneself with patience.

Immersed in shadow and splattered with light, the Marcellus theatre does not look real. Or rather, it has an air of being more real than real life, like the theatre and its stage-settings. This setting can be turned around. Behind it are tables and chairs, a kitchen, a bedroom. These venerable walls still shelter living men. In Rome the past and the present are married and get along well together but it is an eternal triangle in this case: ancient Rome, the classic Rome of great churches and ornate façades, contemporary Rome and its apartment houses. Builders! Builders! It is said that as building goes so goes the nation.

way was built thanks to a bequest by one of Louis XIV's ambassadors.

This is a neighborhood dear to the French since we are already standing in the shade of the Villa Medici where the winners of the Prix de Rome come to live for three years. Roman palaces are imposing but the villas, which are palaces in gardens, are full of grace and nobility. The Villa Medici and the Villa Borghese with its immense park make the Pincio district an enchantment. The Villa Borghese houses a museum where masterpieces abound.

Chateaubriand has fixed in our minds a romantic picture of Via Appia which remains eloquent with its melancholy background of green oaks and cypress-trees. On each side we see tombs and, now and then, an entrance to the catacombs where the early Christians buried their dead to which have recently been added the Cave Ardeatine, horrible caves where the Germans massacred three hundred and thirty-five hostages in 1944.

We have seen the "tituli" in Rome, now let us visit the underground cemeteries from the time of the persecutions. The first are the San Callisto catacombs, four floors of galleries containing the tombs of several popes and that of Saint Cecilia, all decorated with paintings similar to those to be seen in Pompeii, and occasionally frescoes of Byzantine inspiration which were added in the seventh or eighth century.

In the Jewish catacombs dating from the third, fourth and fifth centuries the seven-branch candelabrum is found everywhere.

And now we are passing in front of San-Sebastiano, one of the first basilicas, which also possesses catacombs but it is more important to go down into those of Domitilla for there we will see a hypogeum of the first century with Pompeian-type

Piazza di Spagna, the stairway and church form a perfect image of happiness — with just the right amount of grandeur. Happiness without grandeur is a little happiness. A little happiness is not real happiness. And grandeur without gentleness is not happiness either. Here grandeur and gentleness are equally balanced on the two plates of the scales. This stairway is a French work. This is said with no little pride. These long steps, as long as waves, invite repose. Strangely enough, the car which is passing looks like a ghost. Poor man, where are you hurrying to behind your steering wheel? Towards what business matter which will only give you a lot of work? To what date which will only bring you worries? Stop your chariot. Sit down here. Look at the foreground where all ages of life are represented: the old man contemplating his lost youth, the woman who is looking with self-assurance on age, the other woman, the younger one who is waiting, the young man who is hoping, the adolescent who is admiring his elder. At rest, meditating or thinking of nothing at all, man recaptures his dignity.

frescoes and another from the same period where the niches are decorated with symbols of life and a picture of Daniel. Right next to them, frescoes from the third or fourth century depict Jesus and the Apostles, the Adoration of the Magi, and a wheat market. The Christian paintings have different subjects but remain faithful to pagan techniques.

We pass now in front of the Massenzio circus and arrive at the famous tomb of Cecilia Metalla, a large cylindrical tower which the Caetani transformed into a dungeon, encircling it with a wall which enclosed a castle and a church, the remains of which are still visible.

Starting here the Via Appia recovers its character. The houses have disappeared, leaving only the tombs and trees with silhouettes of aquaducts out on the plain. Certain tombs deserve to be especially admired. A little farther on, there is a farm to visit where the ruins of the Quintilii villa are scattered about. Then we reach Casal Rotondo, the largest of Via Appia's tombs. Finally, five miles away at Torre Selce we discover a pyramid-shaped tumulus on top of which a tower was built in the Middle Ages.

It is a melancholy walk and yet isn't this habit of lining the roads which lead to the city of the living with the tombs of the dead a way of keeping the dead in the midst of life?

It is, moreover, one of Rome's great lessons : the persisting presence of the past in everyday life. Rome has kept vibrant and colorful all the aspects which have characterized its different metamorphoses. Each of them dons its most seductive charms to retain us, and according to our tastes and moods we are enraptured by ancient Rome, early Christian Rome, Renaissance Rome or Baroque Rome, but all these Romes are really only one— the one we want to see again no sooner have we taken leave of it.

We have arrived at the baths and it might be said that we have gotten ourselves into hot water. A strange place. Curious pavement patterned like the sea, evoking the roughness of water and its waves rather than the gentle caress of a bath.

U nder the electric lights
with their wan reflections
which are more silver than
gold, the Galleria becomes
an ambiguous, shady tem-
ple. Shadows glide about
murmuring strange incan-
tations : dollars, French
francs... It is here that
you will find the money
changers. At the right
and more out in the open
about it, the Trevi Foun-
tain waits its cut. Leg-
end has it that you have
only to throw a coin in
the fountain of Trevi to
be assured of returning
to Rome another day.

THE GREAT HOURS IN ROME'S HISTORY

Circa 1000 B.C.

First known inhabitants of Roman region.

Circa 800 B.C.

Foundation of Roman Forum's cemetery, the oldest known Roman monument.

754-753 B.C.

Rome is founded by ROMULUS who, according to legend, traces with his plough the limits of "Roma quadrata" (square Rome) on Palatine Hill.

716 B.C.

Beginning of mythical period of kings.

670-630 B.C.

Reign (according to legend) of TULLUS HOSTILIUS, during which time took place the battle of the HORACES and the CURIACES.

578 B.C.

SERVIUS TULLIUS puts an end to Etruscan tyranny, establishes census, civil status, monetary system. He enclosed Rome within a large wall.

510 B.C.

The Republic is proclaimed after TARQUINIUS SUPERBUS is overthrown by the aristocracy.

493 B.C.

The plebeians take refuge on the sacred hill to escape patrician tyranny. Following this event the tribunes are appointed.

450 B.C.

The Decemvirs set up the Twelve Tables : first Roman written legislation.

445 B.C.

Plebeians obtain right to marry into patrician families, thus establishing civil equality.

439 B.C.

CINCINNATUS' dictatorship.

409-400 B.C.

Plebeians accession to Senate and magistratures.

390 B.C.

Victory of Gauls over Romans at the Battle of Allia. Rome is sacked by BRENNUS who, after a seven-month siege, agrees to leave in exchange for one thousand pounds of gold. Adding the weight of his sword to the scales he shouts, "Vae victis !" ("Woe to the vanquished !").

312 B.C.

Consul Appius CLAUDIUS has the Via Appia laid out and paved.

270 B.C.

Taranto is conquered and Rome is henceforth master of all Italy.

261-241 B.C.

First of three Punic Wars against Carthage

219-201 B.C.

Second Punic War. In 202 HANNIBAL is defeated by SCIPIO AFRICANUS at Zama.

205 B.C.

Spain becomes a Roman province.

168 B.C.

Egypt becomes a Roman province.

146 B.C.

End of Punic Wars and destruction of Carthage. Macedonia and Greece become Roman provinces.

113 B.C.

First Barbarian expedition against the Empire. (Expedition of the Cimbri and Teutons.)

101 B.C.

MARIUS' triumphal entrance into Rome. Birth of JULIUS CAESAR.

60 B.C.

POMPEY, CAESAR and CRASSUS form first Triumvirate.

51 B.C.

Gaul yields to CAESAR.

48 B.C.

Death of POMPEY.

47 B.C.

Victory of JULIUS CAESAR over PHARNACES II. He writes to the Senate : "Veni, vidi, vici..." ("I came, I saw, I conquered.")

46 B.C.

VERCINGETORIX killed in Mamertine prison. CAESAR has Julian basilica built. After a fire it will be rebuilt by AUGUSTUS.

45 B.C.

JULIUS CAESAR creates the Julian Calendar.

March 15, 44 B.C.

Assassination of JULIUS CAESAR in the Senate. CAESAR seeing BRUTUS, his daggar raised, among the assassins, cries out : "Tu quoque, fili!" ("You, too, my son!")

43 B.C.

Death of CICERO. Second Triumvirate (Octavius, Antony, Lepidus).

31 B.C.

The Battle of Actium gives the Empire to OCTAVIUS who takes the name of AUGUSTUS.

30 B.C.

MARC ANTONY besieged in Alexandria, kills himself with CLEOPATRA.

27 B.C.

Pantheon is built.

19 B.C.

Death of VERGIL. He left unfinished the ENEIDE which he wanted to destroy.

13 B.C.

The MARCELLUS theater, with a seating capacity of 12,000, is completed.

8 B.C.

Death of HORACE and his protector, MAECENAS.

2 B.C.

Brilliant inauguration of AUGUSTUS forum.

14

Ascension of TIBERIUS at the age of 56.

17

Death of historian TITUS LIVIUS who had written of the greatness of Rome.

37-41

Reign of CALIGULA who succeeds TIBERIUS.

42

During the reign of CLAUDIUS, SAINT PETER comes to Rome for the first time.

54

Ascension of NERO who succeeds CLAUDIUS.

55

Birth in Umbria of the historian TACITUS.

64

Burning of Rome. NERO blames the Christians for it. He begins construction of his extraordinary "House of Gold".

67

SAINT PETER, after emprisonment in the Mamertine prison, is crucified in the NERO circus. The same day SAINT PAUL is beheaded on the Ostia road.

68

NERO kills himself. On dying he says, "What a great artist perishes with me!"

69

Ascension of VESPASIAN.

79

Ascension of TITUS nicknamed "The delight of the human race".

80

Construction of the Colosseum (begun under VESPASIAN) is completed.

81

The TITUS Arch. The emperor dies in Sabine.

94

The VESPASIAN temple is dedicated to the worship of the deified emperor.

96

Ascension of NERVA, the first of seven ANTONIUSES who will reign until 192.

98-117

Brilliant reign of TRAJAN. In 114 the TRAJAN forum is completed.

117

Ascension of ADRIAN. He had his tomb constructed on the banks of the Tiber, now the Sant'Angelo castle, and in the Roman countryside near Tivoli, the Villa Adriana where, to perpetuate the memory of the most striking places he had seen during his travels in Greece and Egypt, his architects reproduced in miniature monuments like the Athenian Pœcile, the Canopus canal and even Hades according to the poets' notions of it.

128

Beginning of peaceful reign of ANTONIUS PIUS, step father of MARCUS AURELIUS.

161

Ascension of MARCUS AURELIUS.

180

Death of MARCUS AURELIUS. Beginning of a period of decadence.

203

SEPTIMIUS SEVERUS returns from the Orient. The Arch of the sacred Holy Way dedicated to his victory.

211

Ascension of CARACALLA who has baths built in 212, and is assassinated in 217.

284

Ascension of DIOCLETIAN, restorer of the Empire. He applies the Tetrarchy system.

306

MAXENTIUS begin construction of CONSTANTINE basilica on the Sacred Way.

313

CONSTANTINE, by the Edict of Milan, gives Christians the same rights as pagans.

323

Conversion of CONSTANTINE to Christianity.

324

CONSTANTINE builds San Giovanni in Laterano and Santa-Agnese churches.

326

At the request of Pope SYLVESTER I, CONSTANTINE has NERO's circus destroyed and a basilica dedicated to SAINT PETER built on the site.

330

Byzantium takes the name of Constantinople and becomes the capital of the Empire.

337

Death of CONSTANTINE.

352

The Pope SAINT LIBERIO builds the Santa-Maria-Maggiore basilica.

379

Ascension of THEODOSIUS I (THE GREAT) who makes Christianity the official religion of the Empire.

386

VALENTINIAN II constructs SAINT PAUL'S basilica.

410

Rome taken by ALARIC, king of Visigoths.

423

Death of HONORIUS, Emperor of the Occident who had moved the capital of the Empire to Ravenna.

455

Rome sacked by the Vandals.

498

Construction of the Vatican is begun.

579-590

Reign of PELAGIUS II who puts an end to the schism of Milan. He has San Lorenzo fuori le Mura reconstructed and enlarged.

590-604

GREGORY THE GREAT takes the title of Sovereign-Pontiff.

754

PEPIN LE BREF comes to Italy to fight the Lombards and the Byzantines. Beginning of temporal power of Pope (STEVEN II).

Christmas 800

CHARLEMAGNE is crowned Emperor of the Occident by Pope LEO III in Saint Peter's.

822

The present day church of SANTA PRASSEDE is built by PASQUALE I who will hire mosaicists from Ravenna.

846

The Saracens sack Rome.

847-855

Reign of SAINT LEO (LEO IV) who fortifies the Vatican, hence the name "Leonine City".

1073-1095

Investiture quarrel. Pope GREGORY VII struggles with the emperors for supremacy.

1084

ROBERT GUISCARD and his Norman soldiers lay waste to Rome.

1150

EUGENE III begins construction of new Vatican, the former having fallen into ruin.

1155

FREDERICK BARBAROSSA becomes king of Italy. He has the reformer ARNAUD DE BRESCIA killed.

1300

DANTE is received by BONIFACE VIII as ambassador of the Republic of Florence.

1308

The Laterano palace, residence of the popes, is completely destroyed by fire.

1309

At the request of PHILIPPE LE BEL, Pope CLEMENT V leaves Rome and goes to live in Avignon.

1341

PETRARCH is called to Rome to become poet laureate.

1354

The Roman tribune COLA DI RIENZI (or better yet RIENZO) is killed in a riot.

1377

Return of the popes to Rome. GREGORY XI lives in the Vatican which, for the first time, becomes the papal residence.

1445

Beginning of construction of Venezia palace.

1450

Reconstruction of the Constantine basilica which, little by little, will become Saint Peter's basilica as we know it today : ROSSELLINO, BRAMANTE, CARLO MADERNO and BERNINI successively apply their genius to the accomplishment of this masterpiece.

1471

Ascension of Pope SIXTUS IV who has Sistine Chapel built.

1480-1490

Stay in Rome of PERUGINO while he works on Sistine Chapel.

1492

Ascension of Pope ALEXANDER VI BORGIA.

1494

The French king CHARLES VIII orders construction of the Trinità dei Monti church which is today connected with the French Sacré-Cœur convent, famous religious education organization.

1496

MICHELANGELO stays in Rome for the first time.

1497

ALEXANDER VI excommunicates SAVONAROLA who had accused the Pope of being the worst example of ecclesiastical impurity.

1498

MICHELANGELO creates the "*Pietà*" for the Saint Peter basilica.

1500

COPERNICUS teaches mathematics in Rome.

1503

Ascension of Pope JULIUS II, protector of MICHELANGELO. He commissions him to design his tomb and founds the Vatican Museum.

1508

RAPHAEL, age 25, is commissioned by JULIUS II to decorate the "Stanze" of the Vatican. Michelangelo begins work on the frescoes in the Sistine Chapel which he will finish in 1512.

1511

MARTIN LUTHER, age 28, arrives in Rome.

1512

Beginning of construction of Farnese palace.

1513

Ascension of Pope Leo X, protector of arts, letters and sciences.

1516

LEO X signs the Concordat which the French king FRANCES I. RAPHAEL is appointed superintendent of buildings.

1523

Ascension of Pope CLEMENT VII (JULIUS DE MEDICIS). He will refuse to authorize the divorce of HENRY VIII, king of England, thus provoking the Anglican schism.

1527

CHARLES DE BOURBON, High Constable, sacks Rome. CLEMENT takes refuge in the Sant' Angelo castle during the siege.

1536

Entrance of CHARLES V of spain into Rome. MICHELANGELO is commissioned to embellish the Capitol.

1540

Cardinal RICCI DI MONTEPULCIANO has the Villa Medici built following the plan of ANNIBAL LIPPI.

1564

Death of MICHELANGELO. The cupola of San Pietro di Roma will be completed in 1590 by his successor, GIACOMO DELLA PORTA.

1570

Construction of the church of "Gesu", the Jesuits' principal church in Rome.

1574

Construction of the Quirinale is begun, designed by FLAMINIO PONZIO.

1582

GREGORY XIII creates the Gregorian calendar.

1586

Construction of the present Laterano palace.

1595

TASSO dies in the San Onofrio convent in Rome at the moment when the Pope was going to make him laureate in the Capitol.

1615

Construction of Villa Borghese.

1623

Ascension of URBAN VIII, first protector of BERNINI.

1624

NICOLAS POUSSIN arrives in Italy. MADERNO builds the Barberini palace.

1625

CLAUDE LORRAIN leaves Rome. He will return in 1627.

1636

CLAUDE LORRAIN paints in Rome one of his masterpieces : "View of the Port at Sunrise".

1643

NICOLAS POUSSIN paints "The Rapture of Saint Paul".

1647

BERNINI designs the plans for the Piazza Navona fountain.

1665

Death of NICOLAS POUSSIN who is buried in the San Lorenzo in Lucina church.

1666

COLBERT founds the "French Academy in Rome" in the Mancini palace.

1680

Death of BERNINI.

1725

The French Ambassador to Rome commissions the building of the large Piazza di Spagna stairway which leads to the Trinità dei Monti church.

1735

The Trevi fountain is built on CLEMENT XII's order. It is traditional to throw a coin in the fountain to be assured of returning to Rome another day.

1760

Beginning of Greco Café, one of the most famous in Europe along with the Procope in Paris and the Florian in Venice. Right up to our time it will be the favorite meeting place of foreign artists : GOETHE, GOLDONI, BYRON, STENDHAL, LISZT, WAGNER, COROT, GOUNOD, among others, went there frequently.

1786-1788

GOETHE's voyage in Italy. The long stay he made in Rome had a determining influence on his talent, converting him to classicism.

1797

The French Directory forms the Cisalpine Republic.

1801

Signing of the Concordat between PIUS VII and the First Consul.

1802

STENDHAL's first stay in Rome.

1803

"The French Academy in Rome" is transferred from the Mancini palace to Villa Medici. CHATEAUBRIAND's first stay in Rome.

1804

PIUS VII leaves Rome to go to crown NAPOLEON BONAPARTE in Notre-Dame de Paris.

1807

MADAME DE STAEL publishes "*Corinne or Italy*". Birth of GIUSEPPE GARIBALDI in Nice

1809

NAPOLEON annexes Rome to the French Empire.

1811

Birth of NAPOLEON I's son, called King of Rome, in the Tuileries palace.

1814

Return of PIUS VII after NAPOLEON's defeat. He reestablishes the Jesuit order.

1821

Death of JOHN KEATS in Rome.

1822

SHELLEY drowns in the Spezia Gulf. He is buried in the Protestant cemetery in Rome, near KEAT's tomb.

1823

A terrible fire destroys the San Paolo fuori le Mura basilica which is immediately reconstructed by LEO XII.

1828

CHATEAUBRIAND is named ambassador to Rome. In honor of NICOLAS POUSSIN he has a stele designed by the architect VAUDOYER erected in the San Lorenzo in Lucina church.

1831

MAZZINI creates in Marseille the association of "Giovana Italia". STENDHAL, appointed French Consul at Cività Vecchia, returns to his beloved Rome. At the end of the day he would go up to the Pincio to watch the sunset, Saint Peter's dome "outlined on the pastel so pure of a summer twilight".

1834

INGRES is appointed director of the "French Academy in Rome".

1843

COROT's visit. The painters of the Villa Medici make fun of his painting directly from nature but they appreciate the good voice and high spirits of the young artist during evenings spent with young art students at the Greco Café.

1846

Ascension of Pope PIUS IX who becomes the great hope of the partisans of Italian unification. In reality, he will fail for it will be impossible for him to declare war on the greatest Catholic power : Austria.

1847

CAVOUR founds the newspaper *Il Risorgimento* to work towards the rebirth of Italy.

1848

The Roman Republic is set up by GIUSEPPE MAZZINI. PIUS IX flees to Gaeta.

1849

Fall of MAZZINI's Roman Republic in spite of the aid given by GARIBALDI and his legion. The Imperial French Army assures the protection of the Pope.

1860

The Church States are annexed to Sardinia.

1862

Failure of GARIBALDI's "March on Rome". He is arrested by Italian troops at Aspromonte.

1863

Birth of GABRIELE D'ANNUNZIO at Francaville del Mare.

1865

TAINE publishes his "*Voyage in Italy*".

1867

GARIBALDI tries a third time to take Rome. He is arrested by the French at Mentone.

1869

Council of the Vatican when PIUS IX proclaims the dogma of pontifical infallibility.

1870

Rome becomes the capital of Italy. The king moves into the Quirinale Palace.

1878

Death of PIUS IX. Ascension of LEO XIII, "The workers' Pope".

1900

HUMBERT I, son of VICTOR-EMMANUEL II is assassinated at Monza. His son will reign under the name of VICTOR-EMMANUEL III. *La Tosca* by PUCCINI is a great success at the Opera in Rome.

1903

Visit of EDWARD VII of England. Death of LEO XIII. Election of PIUS X.

1914

MARCONI is elected senator to the Italian parliament. Death of PIUS X.

1922

March of the fascist militia on Rome. MUSSOLINI sets up a totalitarian regime.

1929

Laterno Treaty between Pope PIUS XI and MUSSOLINI, recognizing the Pope's temporal sovereignty in Vatican City.

1938

Death of GABRIELE D'ANNUNZIO.

1939

Election of PIUS XII.

1943

Fall of MUSSOLINI.

1946

Abdication of VICTOR-EMMANUEL III and of his son, HUMBERT II. Proclamation of the Republic.

1947-1948

Construction of the "Roma Termini", a former project of the fascist regime. This station, one of the most beautiful in the world, counts among the most remarkable accomplishments of post-war Italy.

1954

Canonization of PIUS X.

1957

Voyage of the French President COTY.

PRINTED IN FRANCE THE 31 OF MAI 1964 THE HÉLIO-GRAVURE WAS PRINTED BY BRAUN OF MULHOUSE AND THE ILLUSTRATIONS IN COLOR BY DRAEGER OF PARIS